GW00976503

Year of Faith

Stations of the Cross

by
Rev Professor Brendan Leahy

*All booklets are published thanks to the
generous support of the members of the
Catholic Truth Society*

CATHOLIC TRUTH SOCIETY
PUBLISHERS TO THE HOLY SEE

Contents

All rights reserved. First published 2013 by The Incorporated Catholic Truth Society, 40-46 Harleyford Road London SE11 5AY Tel: 020 7640 0042 Fax: 020 7640 This edition © The Incorporated Catholic Truth Society 2013.

ISBN 978 1 86082 846 1

Introduction

Early in Christian history, pilgrims in Jerusalem travelled the traditional route from Pilate's house to Calvary. Later, especially in the second millennium, the practice grew up of re-imagining that journey in prayerful recollection at home or in churches. Mulling over its many dimensions and implications, Christians contemplated the purpose for which Jesus of Nazareth went through such a suffering, culminating even in feeling abandoned by God. The Creed provided light - "For our sake he was crucified... suffered death and was buried". To give us God, Jesus felt abandoned by God. To give us light, he was immersed in darkness. To give us justice, he experienced injustice. To give us communion with God and with one another in the Holy Spirit, Jesus knew radical solitude.

When we enter a Catholic church today, a feature of its architecture - sometimes discreet, sometimes more obvious - are signs, carvings or images, generally along the side walls called "Stations of the Cross". They are designed to prompt the mind's eye to perceive Jesus' journey to Calvary and so contemplate it, step by step, especially during Lent and on Good Friday. In doing so, sentiments of gratitude arise when believers reflect on how much love is expressed in Jesus, the God with a human,

4

suffering face. Not only that, but in following the Stations, believers move from gratitude to entrustment - entrusting their lives, the lives of others and the complex situations around us to this infinite, merciful and immense love.

Above all, perhaps, new or renewed proposals of fidelity are formulated as we move from Station to Station - to be a worthy response to Jesus' suffering and death by allowing ourselves, and today's world, to be brought with him into the new life of the Resurrection, the gift of salvation, fruit of Jesus' death. The Creed affirms: "For our sake he...rose again on the third day...ascended into heaven and is seated at the right hand of the Father". While we "look forward to the resurrection of the dead and the life of the world to come", the life of the Resurrection is not just for when we die. It already begins now for us in faith. It can already now have an impact in economics and politics, education and family life.

The Resurrection has indeed, as Pope Benedict puts it, opened up "a dimension that affects us all, creating for all of us a new space of life, a new space of being in union with God",[1] a space of light and life, love and unity. It is the space opened up by the risen Jesus who wants us to feel his life-giving presence among us when we gather in his name: "For where two or three meet in my name, I am there among them" (*Mt* 18:20).

---

[1] *Jesus of Nazareth*, Holy Week, p. 274.

The Year of Faith

Every day is a chance to deepen our faith. The mystery of death and resurrection is written into the very rhythm of our faith that works through love. To believe is to entrust myself to God who has revealed himself in Jesus Christ and, in the power of the Spirit, to enter through him into the community of the Church. It is in the measure to which we let ourselves be transformed by the Crucified Christ - in our thoughts and affections, mentality and conduct - that we enter into the radical new reality of communion with Christ that opens up in the Resurrection. The expression of this new life is to be found day by day in our relationships of communion with one another. Yes, faith is a great gift, not to be limited to a corner of my life, but rather to be lived out in building up a new humanity of peace and justice, truth and solidarity.

In the centuries-old tradition of the Stations of the Cross we are given a chance to contemplate all of this. The traditional set of fourteen Stations was recognised by Pope Clement XII in 1731. In 1991 Pope John Paul II used a more directly Scripture-based set of the Stations. But in general recent Popes have followed the traditional fourteen. The value of this fourteen is to be found, not least, in that three of the Stations invite us to meditate directly on the role of the women who accompanied Jesus. By extension they remind us of the many women throughout the centuries of the Church who have witnessed in countless ways to the Gospel. Since the Second Vatican Council, a concluding fifteenth Station is often introduced as a meditation on the Resurrection and this booklet has followed suit.[2]

These Stations were first celebrated during an Easter retreat for priests and seminarians at St Patrick's College, Maynooth to whom I dedicate this short text in gratitude. In this publication I have added some short passages from the *Catechism of the Catholic Church* to accompany personal reflection on each Station.

(Brendan Leahy)

---

[2] Biblical quotations are taken from *The New Jerusalem Bible* (London: Darton, Longman & Todd, 1985).

Opening Prayer

Lord, you were condemned to death because fear of what others may think suppressed the voice of conscience.

How many times have we ourselves preferred success to the truth, our reputation to justice? Strengthen the quiet voice of our conscience that is your own voice in our lives. Let your gaze penetrate our hearts and indicate the direction our lives must take.

(Benedict XVI)

1. Jesus is condemned to Death

V. We adore you, O Christ,
and praise you.

R. Because by your holy Cross,
you have redeemed the world.

"Having loved his own who were in
the world, he loved them to the end."
(*Jn* 13:1)

Straightaway death is put before us in the First Station.
It was always the horizon towards which Jesus walked.
He moved towards "his hour" as John's Gospel calls it.
But now comes the moment when Pilate announces it.
The moment of death's "announcement" will come to
all of us. So it is good, in imitation of Jesus, to decide
to accept our death, whenever, wherever and however
our Lord wants. We can get ready for "our hour" by
dying to ourselves at least a little every day.

Reflection:

'Remembering our mortality helps us realize that we have only a limited time in which to bring our lives to fulfilment... The Church encourages us to prepare ourselves for the hour of our death...to ask the Mother of God to intercede for us "at the hour of our death" in the *Hail Mary*; and to entrust ourselves to St Joseph, the patron of a happy death'.

(*CCC* 1007 and 1014. See further, *CCC* 1005-1019)

Our Father, Hail Mary, Glory be to the Father.

V. Have mercy on us O Lord.

R. Have mercy on us.

May the souls of the faithful departed, through the mercy of God, rest in peace.
Amen.

2. Jesus receives his Cross

V. We adore you, O Christ,
   and praise you.

R. Because by your holy Cross,
   you have redeemed the world.

"If anyone wants to be a follower of
mine, let him renounce himself and
take up his cross and follow me." (*Mt* 16:24)

There is a particular cross for each one of us. Its shape
and size is different for you, for me, for the person next
to you. What's important is to take up the cross, not
drag it. At every Mass we are given an opportunity to
unite our suffering to Jesus' by spiritually adding every
shadow of darkness that we experience or know of in
the world around us to the chalice on the altar at Mass.
When we see the priest pour drops of water into the
chalice, deep down within us, we can say "I give you
all the suffering of today's world; and I give you my
suffering, my personal cross". Every suffering can
acquire value.

Reflection:

For all their [laity's] works, prayers, and apostolic undertakings, family and married life, daily work, relaxation of mind and body, if they are accomplished in the Spirit - indeed even the hardships of life if patiently born - all these become spiritual sacrifices acceptable to God through Jesus Christ. In the celebration of the Eucharist these may most fittingly be offered to the Father along with the body of the Lord.

(*CCC* 901. See further, *CCC* 897-913)

Our Father, Hail Mary, Glory be to the Father.

V. Have mercy on us O Lord.

R. Have mercy on us.

May the souls of the faithful departed, through the mercy of God, rest in peace.
Amen.

3. Jesus falls the first time

V. We adore you, O Christ,
    and praise you.

R. Because by your holy Cross,
    you have redeemed the world.

"Unless a grain of wheat falls into
the earth and dies, it remains alone;
but if it dies, it yields a rich harvest." (*Jn* 12:24)

The occasions when we fall, especially in our day to
day relationships with those we love the most, cause us
pain. A great consolation of faith is to realise that God
can draw good out of all situations of evil, indeed he
can draw more good out of them than all the potential
negative effects those situations have brought about.
Each fall, then, can be an occasion to make a new act
of faith - to believe always in God's immense love,
to believe his love can work where my love fails,
to believe that through our efforts he can intervene
where social conditions might indicate despair. Love
conquers all.

Reflection:

We must therefore approach the question of the origin of evil by fixing the eyes of our faith on him who alone is its conqueror... The victory that Christ won over sin has given us greater blessings than those which sin had taken from us: "where sin increased, grace abounded all the more" (*Rm* 5:20)... And St Thomas Aquinas wrote, "There is nothing to prevent human nature's being raised up to something greater, even after sin; God permits evil in order to draw forth some greater good."

(*CCC* 385, 420 and 412. See further, *CCC* 385-421)

Our Father, Hail Mary, Glory be to the Father.

V. Have mercy on us O Lord.

R. Have mercy on us.

May the souls of the faithful departed, through the mercy of God, rest in peace.
Amen.

4. Jesus meets his mother

V. We adore you, O Christ,
   and praise you.

R. Because by your holy Cross,
   you have redeemed the world.

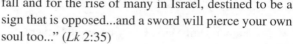

"Then Simeon...said to his mother
Mary, 'Look, he is destined for the
fall and for the rise of many in Israel, destined to be a
sign that is opposed...and a sword will pierce your own
soul too..." (*Lk* 2:35)

Simeon had told Mary when Jesus was only a child that
her son would be a "sign that is opposed", a "sign of
contradiction". So she knew that following him would
involve going against the tide. And yet how alone she
must have been among the crowds of Jerusalem. She
is a model for us when we can be tempted to simply
go with the flow without really evaluating is what I am
doing right? Mary lives out all the virtues that Jesus
embodies: patience, humility, meekness, perseverance,
temperance, and fortitude.

Reflection:

Thus the Blessed Virgin advanced in her pilgrimage of faith, and faithfully persevered in her union with her Son unto the cross. There she stood, in keeping with the divine plan... to be given, by the same Christ Jesus dying on the cross, as a mother to his disciple, with these words: "Woman, behold your son."

(CCC 964 quoting *Lumen Gentium* 58.
See further, *CCC* 963-975)

Our Father, Hail Mary, Glory be to the Father.

V. Have mercy on us O Lord.

R. Have mercy on us.

May the souls of the faithful departed, through the mercy of God, rest in peace.
Amen.

5. Simon helps Jesus to carry his Cross

V. We adore you, O Christ,
    and praise you.

R. Because by your holy Cross,
    you have redeemed the world.

"The whole of the Law is summarised
in the one commandment: 'You must
love your neighbour as yourself'
… Carry each other's burdens…'"(*Ga* 5:14 and *Ga* 6:2)

Getting up that morning little could Simon have
imagined he would have to come to the aid of a
"neighbour" in Jerusalem that day, a neighbour called
Jesus carrying his Cross. Each neighbour around me is
a presence of Jesus for me. It's not that I "have" to help
my neighbour, but it is my dignity that I "can" give
a hand out of love. Jesus is there in each neighbour
waiting for me because each person is, in a mysterious
way, linked to the one mystical body of Christ and so
another "me" to be loved as myself.

Reflection:

The *works of mercy* are charitable actions by which we come to the aid of our neighbour in his spiritual and bodily necessities. Instructing, advising, consoling, comforting are spiritual works of mercy, as are forgiving and bearing wrongs patiently. The corporal works of mercy consist especially in feeding the hungry, sheltering the homeless, clothing the naked, visiting the sick and imprisoned, and burying the dead.

(CCC 2447. See further, CCC 2443-2457)

Our Father, Hail Mary, Glory be to the Father.

V. Have mercy on us O Lord.

R. Have mercy on us.

May the souls of the faithful departed, through the mercy of God, rest in peace.
Amen.

6. Veronica wipes the face of Jesus

V. We adore you, O Christ,
   and praise you.

R. Because by your holy Cross,
   you have redeemed the world.

"I tell you, in so far as you did this to
one of the least…you did it to me."
(*Mt* 25:40)

Tradition tells us that Veronica wiped Jesus' face and
the image (the name "Veronica" means "true icon")
was impressed on the cloth she used. The image of
Jesus I see in the neighbour who passes me by in the
present moment of life is always different, perhaps
Jesus who has to be helped to be born and to grow, to
hear a word of encouragement and frank correction, or
to be supported in order to die to him/herself and to
rise again. But it is always Jesus. Each person is on a
different moment of life's journey and to be loved in
the way best for him or her at this moment. No one
should pass me by in vain.

Reflection:

Being in the image of God the human individual possesses the dignity of a person, who is not just something, but someone. He is capable of self-knowledge, of self-possession and of freely giving himself and entering into communion with other persons.

(*CCC* 357. See further, *CCC* 355-379)

Our Father, Hail Mary, Glory be to the Father.

V. Have mercy on us O Lord.

R. Have mercy on us.

May the souls of the faithful departed, through the mercy of God, rest in peace.
Amen.

7. Jesus falls the second time

V. We adore you, O Christ,
   and praise you.

R. Because by your holy Cross,
   you have redeemed the world.

"For it is when I am weak that I am
strong." (*2 Co* 12:10)

The logic of the Gospel is one of paradox. Because of
Jesus' death and resurrection, we can say that those who
lose their lives save them, death is life, and weakness
is strength. In this logic, every fall can become an
experience of new life - if I allow redemption work its
effect in me. Yes, because in the Gospel logic of paradox,
every failure and difficulty - at home, at college, in
the office, in a relationship, in the neighbourhood -
contains a hidden redemptive power that can make of
all negative occasions a springboard, launching me to
be the first to love, to take the initiative in reaching out,
to expand my heart in care of others, in short, to let the
redemption work in me, in today's world.

Reflection:

By giving up his own Son for our sins, God manifests that his plan for us is one of benevolent love... At the end of the parable of the lost sheep Jesus recalled that God's love excludes no one... The Church, following the apostles, teaches that Christ died for all men without exception: "There is not, never has been, and never will be a single human being for whom Christ did not suffer."

(CCC 604-605. See further, *CCC* 599-623)

Our Father, Hail Mary, Glory be to the Father.

V. Have mercy on us O Lord.

R. Have mercy on us.

May the souls of the faithful departed, through the mercy of God, rest in peace.
Amen.

8. Jesus meets the women of Jerusalem

V. We adore you, O Christ,
and praise you.

R. Because by your holy Cross,
you have redeemed the world.

"A woman in childbirth suffers
because her time has come.
But when she has given birth to the child she forgets
the suffering…" (*Jn* 16:21)

The Church is Jesus Christ's mystical body. He
generated it on the Cross. It is significant that this
Station presents us with Jesus on the way to the Cross
meeting the women of Jerusalem. It is the women who
remain with Jesus to the end. They echo Mary's "yes"
said from the beginning of Jesus' earthly life. There is
a feminine "yes" of love, of holiness, of letting it be,
of truth in love, at the heart of the Church. It makes
up for the shortcomings and the "no" of Peter and the
other disciples.

Reflection:

[The Church's] structure is totally ordered to the holiness of Christ's members. And holiness is measured according to the "great mystery" in which the Bride responds with the gift of love to the gift of the Bridegroom." Mary goes before us all in the holiness that is the Church's mystery... This is why the "Marian" dimension of the Church precedes the "Petrine".

(*CCC* 773. See further, *CCC* 771-780)

Our Father, Hail Mary, Glory be to the Father.

V. Have mercy on us O Lord.

R. Have mercy on us.

May the souls of the faithful departed, through the mercy of God, rest in peace.
Amen.

9. Jesus falls for the third time

V. We adore you, O Christ,
   and praise you.

R. Because by your holy Cross,
   you have redeemed the world.

"He was bearing our sins in his own
body on the cross… Through his
bruises you have been healed." (*1 P* 2:24)

It's discouraging to notice how often I fall. It's easy
to end languishing in a valley of disappointment and
weariness at my personal limits. But for Jesus what
matters is not this or that fall or failure but, to make an
act of hope and live the present moment well. Listen to
St Bernard: those who do not go forward go backwards.
So, I can make a proposal: start again; don't look back,
what's done is done, hand it over to God's mercy. Live
the present moment well. Don't worry about the future
- in hope leave that to God's loving providence. Focus
on the now.

Reflection:

Hope is the theological virtue by which we desire the kingdom of heaven and eternal life as our happiness, placing our trust in Christ's promises and relying not on our own strength, but on the help of the grace of the Holy Spirit. "Let us hold fast the confession of our hope without wavering, for he who promised is faithful."

(*CCC* 1817. See further, *CCC* 1812-1829)

Our Father, Hail Mary, Glory be to the Father.

V. Have mercy on us O Lord.

R. Have mercy on us.

May the souls of the faithful departed, through the mercy of God, rest in peace.
Amen.

10. Jesus is stripped of his garments.

V. We adore you, O Christ,
   and praise you.

R. Because by your holy Cross,
   you have redeemed the world.

   "I was…lacking clothes and you
   clothed me…" (*Mt* 25:36)

In the first chapters of the Bible, we are told that God clothed Adam and Eve. He gave them dignity. Stripped of his garments, Jesus is a symbol of humanity's constant need to be "clothed". By taking on humanity's sinfulness, Jesus' love covered the multitude of our sins. The fruit of this, as St Paul tells us, is that we have been "re-clothed" in Christ with the dignity of the children of God. It's up to us now to continue covering a multitude of sins through our love for one another, helping each other to discover our dignity as children of God - listening well to those who have been deeply wounded, trying to see things from our neighbour's point of view, offering friendship and making room for one another.

Reflection:

> Indeed the sacrament of Reconciliation with God brings about a true "spiritual resurrection", restoration of the dignity and blessings of the life of the children of God, of which the most precious is friendship with God... This sacrament...does not simply heal the one restored to ecclesial communion, but has also a revitalizing effect on the life of the Church...
>
> (*CCC* 1468-1469. See further *CCC* 1440-1470)

Our Father, Hail Mary, Glory be to the Father.

V. Have mercy on us O Lord.

R. Have mercy on us.

May the souls of the faithful departed, through the mercy of God, rest in peace.
Amen.

11. Jesus is nailed to the Cross

V. We adore you, O Christ,
   and praise you.

R. Because by your holy Cross,
   you have redeemed the world.

"The Word became flesh, he lived
among us... Jesus, having loved those
who were his in the world, loved them to the end."
(*Jn* 1:14; *Jn* 13)

The Son of God who lived among us reached the point
of being crucified for us. The God-man is dying for me.
This is friendship. This is more than friendship. It tells
me that God has made me/us the centre of his life: "I
have laid down my life for you". While at this Station
we think especially of all who are suffering physically
at this time, we can also think about the movement of
love that has reached this point. God gave up his Son
for me. Jesus, the Son, gave up his life for me. Mary,
the Mother, standing at the Cross gave up her Son for
me. Now it's up to me to give my life for others. The
links in the movement of love continue.

Reflection:

In all of his life Jesus presents himself as our model...
In humbling himself, he has given us an example to
imitate, through his prayer he draws us to pray, and by
his poverty he calls us to accept freely the privation and
persecutions that may come our way.

(CCC 520. See further, CCC 514-521)

Our Father, Hail Mary, Glory be to the Father.

V. Have mercy on us O Lord.

R. Have mercy on us.

May the souls of the faithful departed, through the
mercy of God, rest in peace.
Amen.

12. Jesus dies on the Cross

V. We adore you, O Christ,
   and praise you.

R. Because by your holy Cross,
   you have redeemed the world.

"Eloi, Eloi, lama sabachthani which
means, 'My God, my God, why have
you forsaken me?'" (*Mk* 15:34)

It is absurd. God is crying out to God! But in Jesus'
question we hear the cry of humanity. And that
question is the answer to all our questions. It tells us
that Jesus has entered into all our "whys" and brought
them into his dialogue with God the Father who cannot
but reply, in his time and in the way he knows best,
to our cry. It is moving to realise how Jesus called
to God the Father with the language of his mother:
"*Eloi, Eloi lama sabachthani?*"

Reflection:

Jesus did not experience reprobation as if he himself had sinned. But in the redeeming love that always united him to the Father, he assumed us in the state of our waywardness of sin, to the point that he could say in our name from the cross: "My God, my God, why have you forsaken me?" Having thus established him in solidarity with us sinners, God "did not spare his own Son but gave him up for us all", so that we might be "reconciled to God by the death of his Son".

(*CCC* 603. See further, *CCC* 599-623)

Our Father, Hail Mary, Glory be to the Father.

V. Have mercy on us O Lord.

R. Have mercy on us.

May the souls of the faithful departed, through the mercy of God, rest in peace.
Amen.

13. Jesus is taken down from the Cross

V. We adore you, O Christ,
and praise you.

R. Because by your holy Cross,
you have redeemed the world.

"And being in the form of God (Jesus)
did not cling to his equality with God
as something to be grasped. But he emptied himself…"
(*Ph* 2: 6-7)

What can I say as I see the dead Jesus being taken down
from the Cross? A prayer in the form of a promise:
Here I am, Jesus, standing before you. I want to live in
a new way, living the Christian life as you want me to
live it, along with all who bear the name of Christian.
I want to be a worthy fruit of your immense love. Here
I am, Lord.

Reflection:

It is by his prayer that Jesus vanquishes the tempter, both at the outset of his public mission and in the ultimate struggle of his agony. In this petition to our heavenly Father ["And lead us not into temptation"], Christ unites us to his battle and his agony. He urges us to vigilance of the heart in communion with his own. Vigilance is "custody of the heart", and Jesus prayed for us to the Father: "Keep them in your name." The Holy Spirit constantly seeks to awaken us to keep watch. Finally, this petition takes on all its dramatic meaning in relation to the last temptation of our earthly battle; it asks for final perseverance.

(*CCC* 2849. See further, *CCC* 2558-2855)

Our Father, Hail Mary, Glory be to the Father.

V. Have mercy on us O Lord.

R. Have mercy on us.

May the souls of the faithful departed, through the mercy of God, rest in peace.
Amen.

14. Jesus is laid in the tomb

V. We adore you, O Christ,
and praise you.

R. Because by your holy Cross,
you have redeemed the world.

"At the place where he had been
crucified there was a garden, and in
this garden a new tomb...they laid
Jesus there." (*Jn* 19:25)

In the stillness of Holy Saturday, Mary emerges as a
monument of holiness. Christ has died, "descended into
hell", spreading his redemptive work to all people of all
times and all places. But the mother stands in that powerful
charity that "bears all things, endures all things, hopes all
things". And a new, expanded maternity, assigned to her
by Jesus, begins as John, representing humanity, takes her
to his home. As my mother, she shows me how my heart
too needs to be expanded in charity in relation to those
around me, and to countless others: my fellow Catholics,
my brother and sister Christians of other denominations,
my neighbours of other world religions, and perhaps
above all, my friends of no religious conviction.

Reflection:

The state of the dead Christ is the mystery of the tomb and the descent into hell. It is the mystery of Holy Saturday, when Christ, lying in the tomb, reveals God's great Sabbath rest after the fulfillment of man's salvation, which brings peace to the whole universe... Baptism, the original and full sign of which is immersion, efficaciously signifies the descent into the tomb by the Christian who dies to sin with Christ in order to live a new life.

(*CCC* 624 and 628. See further, *CCC* 624-630)

Our Father, Hail Mary, Glory be to the Father.

V. Have mercy on us O Lord.

R. Have mercy on us.

May the souls of the faithful departed, through the mercy of God, rest in peace.
Amen.

15. Jesus rises from the dead

V. We adore you, O Christ,
   and praise you.

R. Because by your holy Cross,
   you have redeemed the world.

"He has risen, as he said. Come, see…
then go quickly and tell…" (*Mt* 28:7)

Jesus is Risen. Death does not have the last word. From Easter Sunday onwards, a divine alchemy has been written into our lives and into history: death is swallowed up in victory. Yes, history still runs its course, but there's the deeper story. We need not be blocked in the trauma of sin and division, suffering and death. In the Risen Christ, when we love, we too can "pass over from death to life" (1 *Jn* 3:14). And when two or more of us unite in our love for one another with the measure he has shown us on the Cross, then we can experience among us the presence of the risen Jesus, the author of Life, with his peace and new life, ardour and zeal, building a new humanity.

Reflection:

Christ's Resurrection was not a return to earthly life, as was the case with the raisings from the dead that he had performed before Easter: Jairus' daughter, the young man of Naim, Lazarus. ...At Jesus' Resurrection his body is filled with the power of the Holy Spirit: he shares the divine life in his glorious state... In Christ, Christians "have tasted...the powers of the age to come" and their lives are swept up by Christ into the heart of divine life, so that they may "live no longer for themselves but for him who for their sake died and was raised."

(*CCC* 646 and 655. See further, *CCC* 638-658)

Our Father, Hail Mary, Glory be to the Father.

V. Have mercy on us O Lord.

R. Have mercy on us.

May the souls of the faithful departed, through the mercy of God, rest in peace.
Amen.

Concluding Prayer

Father, around your throne the Saints, our brothers and sisters, sing your praise forever. Their glory fills us with joy, and their communion with us in the Church gives us inspiration and strength as we hasten on our pilgrimage of faith, eager to meet them.